Alphabets - *Sizzling* and **Se**
Gallery of Alphabets - Uppercase A

40+ Alphabets

Sizzling

and

Sensational

Charted for Needlework

by Tink Boord-Dill

TB-DN

ALPHABETS
For Discerning Makers

20th ANNIVERSARY EDITION

The Teal Book

Alphabets – Sizzling and Sensational

Acknowledgments

Much love to my Mom, who is always on my side! I love you, Mom!!!

And to Peg... your grace and courage is always an inspiration to me!

Thank you, Studio Mastiffs, Hercules and Mam'selle, for your endless help and supervision.

Alphabets – Sizzling and Sensational

Dedication

20th Anniversary Edition

As I readied these books for their new editions, visiting each dedication page has been a wonderful walk down memory lane. Some friends are still with us, while others are not. My mother, my greatest support, is now gone, as are all of my wonderful dogs -- My Big Guys. Still here is Jeffrey, Dear Husband, as we approach our 30th Anniversary. Beppi, our retirement dog, is very different from 'My Big Guys' but every day with him is a treasure and delight... Even while imploring, "Don't be that dog!"

⸺⸻⸻⸻⸻⸺

This book is dedicated to my new staff member, Hercules. You are a delight. Thank you for joining our family!

ALPHABETS – Sizzling and Sensational
List of Alphabets

Alphabet Name	Alphabet Number	
Accitte18 Upper Case	Alphabet 1	
Accitte24 Upper Case	Alphabet 2	
Ambiggy20 Upper Case	Alphabet 3	
Arri15 Upper Case	Alphabet 4	
Arri15 Lower Case	Alphabet 5	
Arri20 Upper Case	Alphabet 6	
Arri20 Lower Case	Alphabet 7	
Arri25 Upper Case	Alphabet 8	(2 Graphs)
Arri25 Lower Case	Alphabet 9	
Arrowz18Dark Upper Case	Alphabet 10	
Arrowz18Light Upper Case	Alphabet 11	
Arrowz24Dark Upper Case	Alphabet 12	
Arrowz24Light Upper Case	Alphabet 13	(2 Graphs)
Asianish18 Upper Case	Alphabet 14	
Asianish24 Upper Case	Alphabet 15	(2 Graphs)
BellyDance18 Upper Case	Alphabet 16	
BellyDance18 Lower Case	Alphabet 17	
BellyDance24 Upper Case	Alphabet 18	(2 Graphs)
BellyDance24 Lower Case	Alphabet 19	
Bitter18 Upper Case	Alphabet 20	
Bitter24 Upper Case	Alphabet 21	
Buttercreme18 Upper Case	Alphabet 22	
Buttercreme18 Lower Case	Alphabet 23	
Buttercreme24 Upper Case	Alphabet 24	(2 Graphs)
Buttercreme24 Lower Case	Alphabet 25	(2 Graphs)
HoppieDown18 Upper Case	Alphabet 26	

ALPHABETS – Sizzling and Sensational
List of Alphabets

Alphabet Name	Alphabet Number	
HoppieDown24 Upper Case	Alphabet 27	(2 Graphs)
HoppieUp18 Upper Case	Alphabet 28	
HoppieUp24 Upper Case	Alphabet 29	(2 Graphs)
LicketyNotSplit18 Upper Case	Alphabet 30	
LicketySplit18 Upper Case	Alphabet 31	
Mudgie18 Upper Case	Alphabet 32	
Mudgie18 Lower Case	Alphabet 33	
Mudgie24 Upper Case	Alphabet 34	(2 Graphs)
Mudgie24 Lower Case	Alphabet 35	
Noire15 Upper Case	Alphabet 36	
Noire18 Upper Case	Alphabet 37	
Noire21 Upper Case	Alphabet 38	
Noire24 Upper Case	Alphabet 39	(2 Graphs)
Seggie18 Upper Case	Alphabet 40	
Seggie18 Lower Case	Alphabet 41	
Seggie24 Upper Case	Alphabet 42	
Seggie24 Lower Case	Alphabet 43	
Threez18 Upper Case	Alphabet 44	(2 Graphs)
Threez18 Lower Case	Alphabet 45	(2 Graphs)
Threez24 Upper Case	Alphabet 46	(2 Graphs)
Threez24 Lower Case	Alphabet 47	(2 Graphs)

Designer's Notes
Many times, 2 identical Alphabets of different sizes can be combined as if they were an Upper case and a Lower Case, creating an interesting effect.
All of these Alphabets are suitable for Cross Stitch and most are suitable for Tent Stitch.
Any of the Alphabets can be used in Traditional Needlepoint if stitched using a Cross Stitch.
When doing this, use fewer plies of thread than in Tent Stitch and make sure that the upper stitch follows the same orientation as the Tent Stitches used.

Accitte18 Upper Case

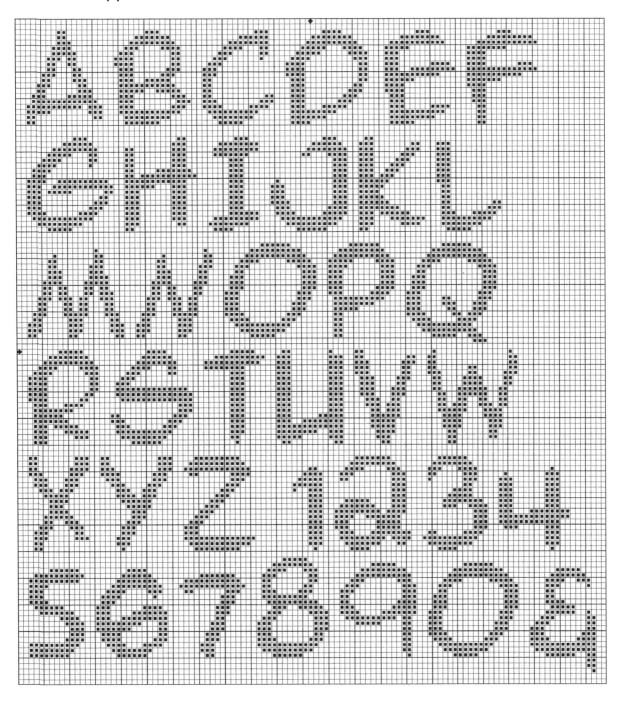

Accitte24 Upper Case

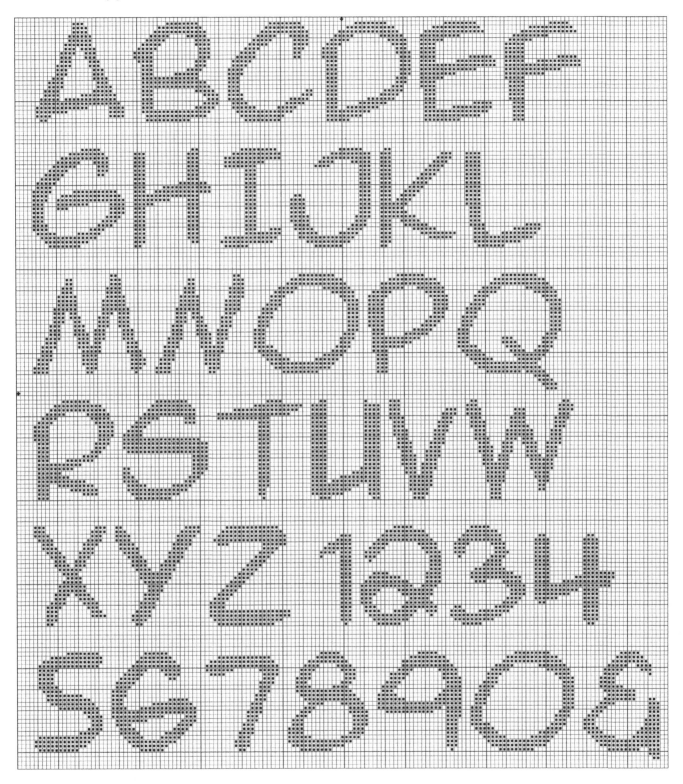

Ambiggy20 Upper Case

Arri15 Upper Case

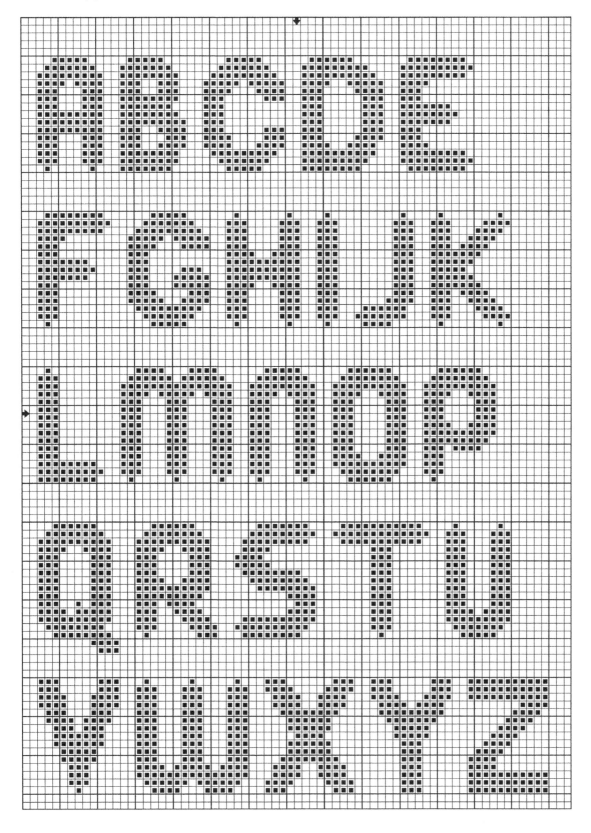

Arri15 Lower Case

Arri20 Upper Case

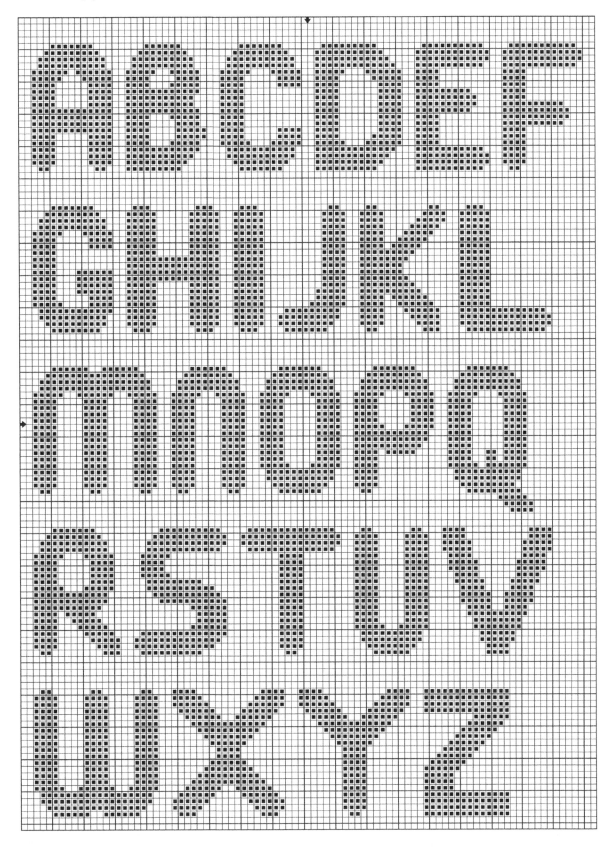

Arri20 Lower Case

Arri25 Upper Case   Graph 1 of 2

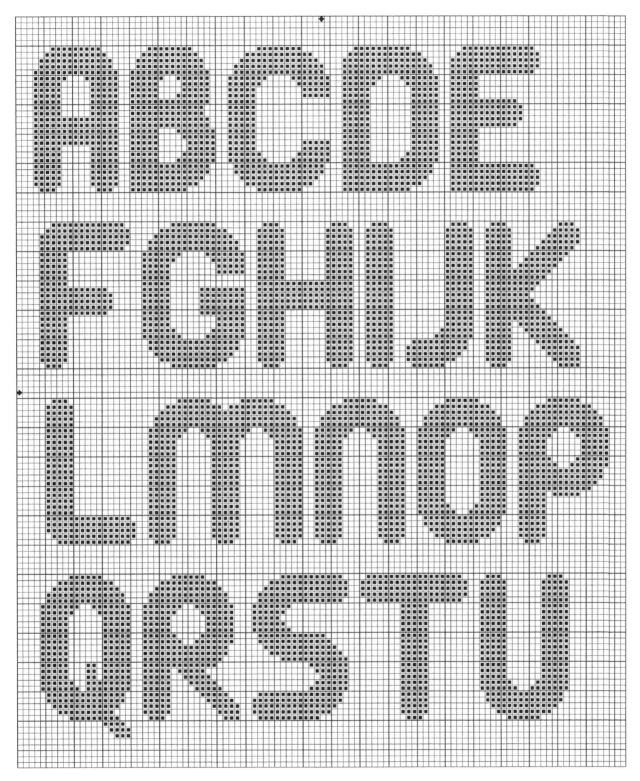

Arri25 Upper Case   Graph 2 of 2

Arri25 Lower Case

Arrowz18Dark Upper Case

Arrowz18Light Upper Case

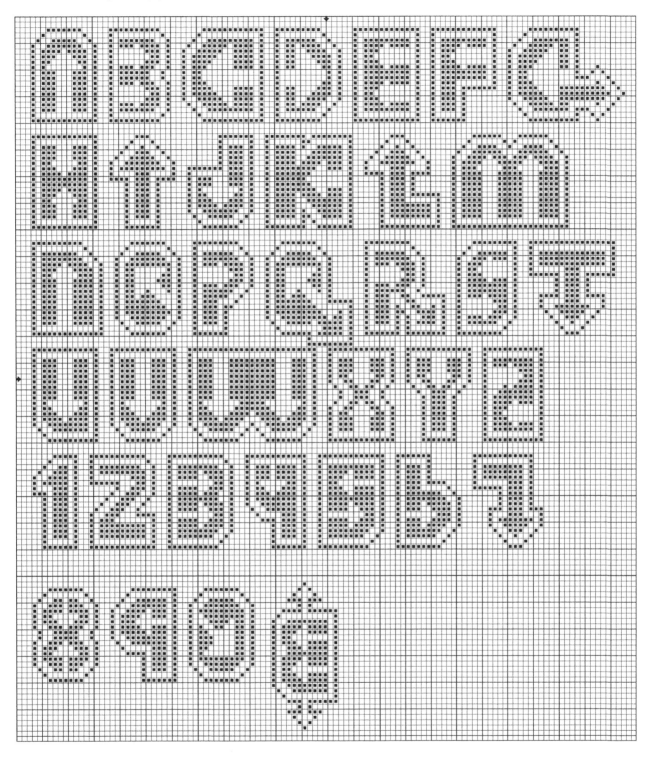

Arrowz24Dark Upper Case

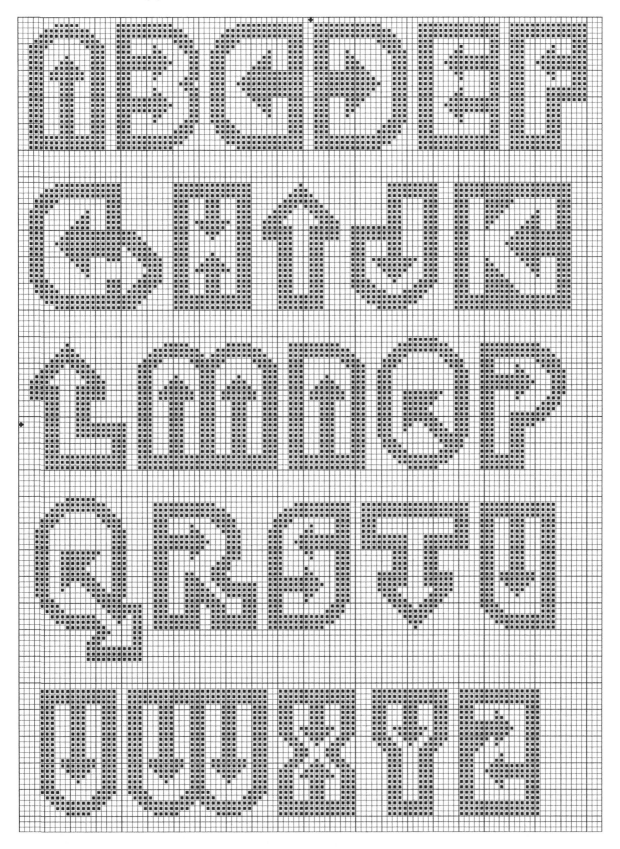

Arrowz24Light Upper Case   Graph 1 of 2

Arrowz24Light Upper Case   Graph 2 of 2

Asianish18 Upper Case

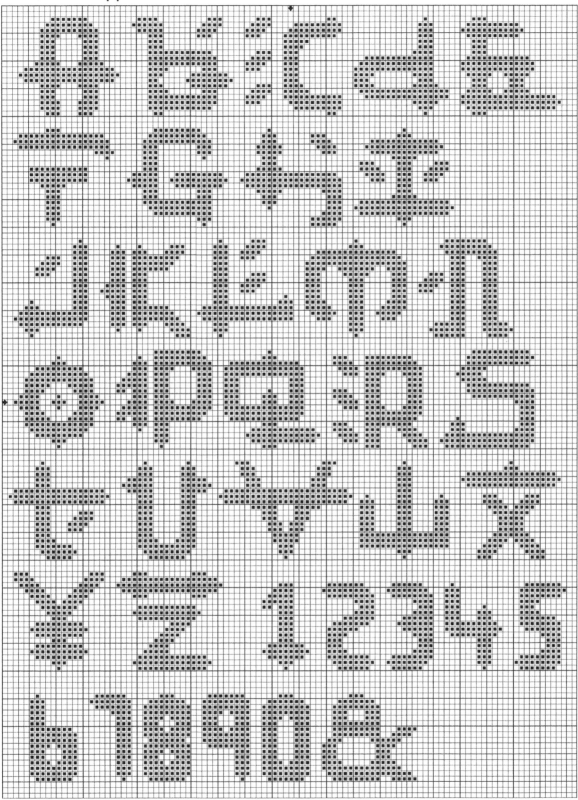

Asianish24 Upper Case   Graph 1 of 2

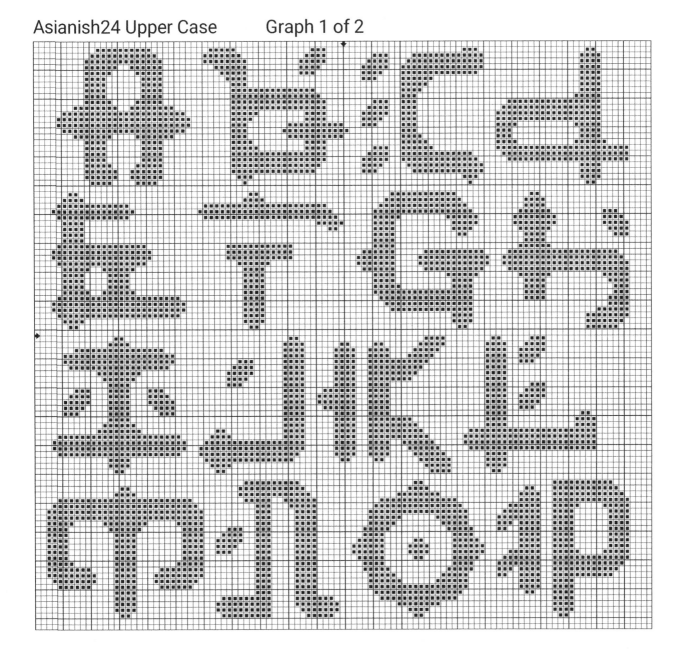

Asianish24 Upper Case   Graph 2 of 2

BellyDance18 Upper Case

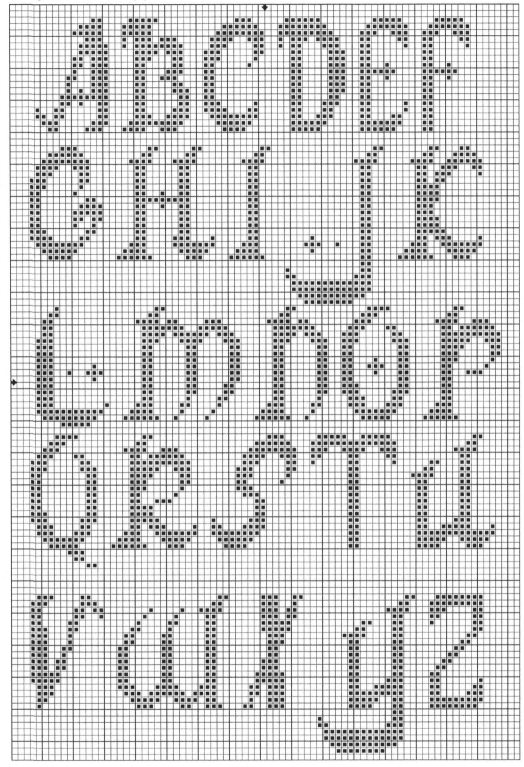

BellyDance18 Lower Case

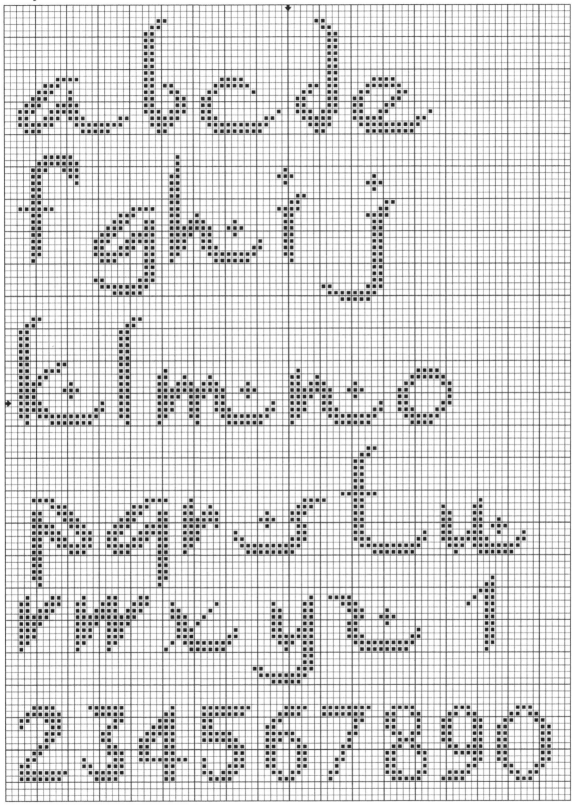

BellyDance24 Upper Case   Graph 1 of 2

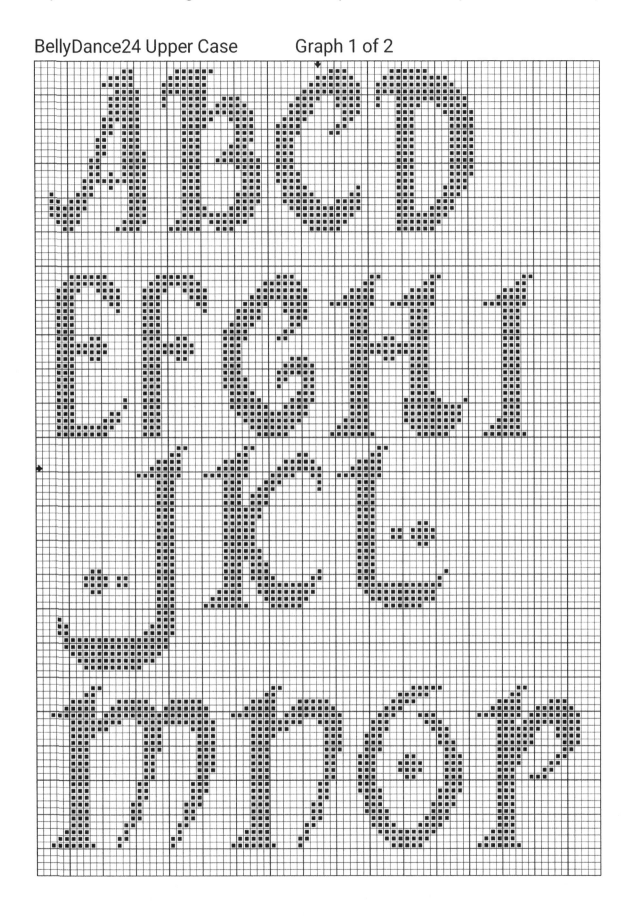

BellyDance24 Upper Case   Graph 2 of 2

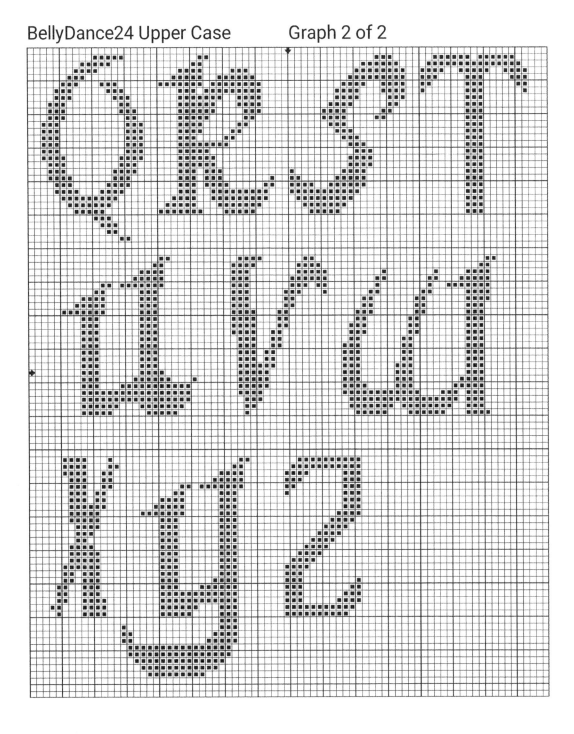

BellyDance24 Lower Case

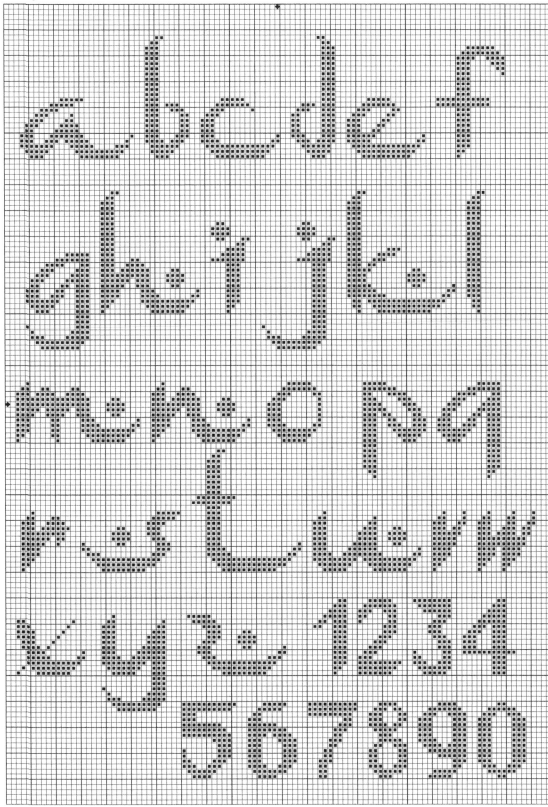

Bitter18 Upper Case

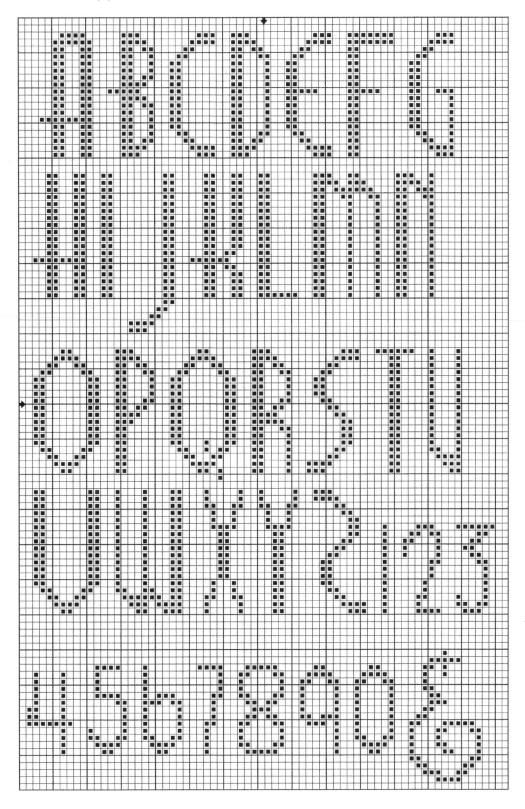

Bitter24 Upper Case

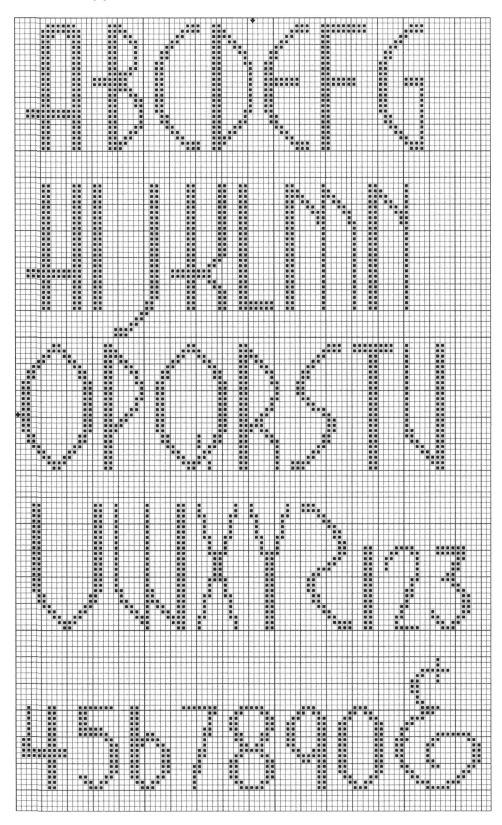

Buttercreme18 Upper Case

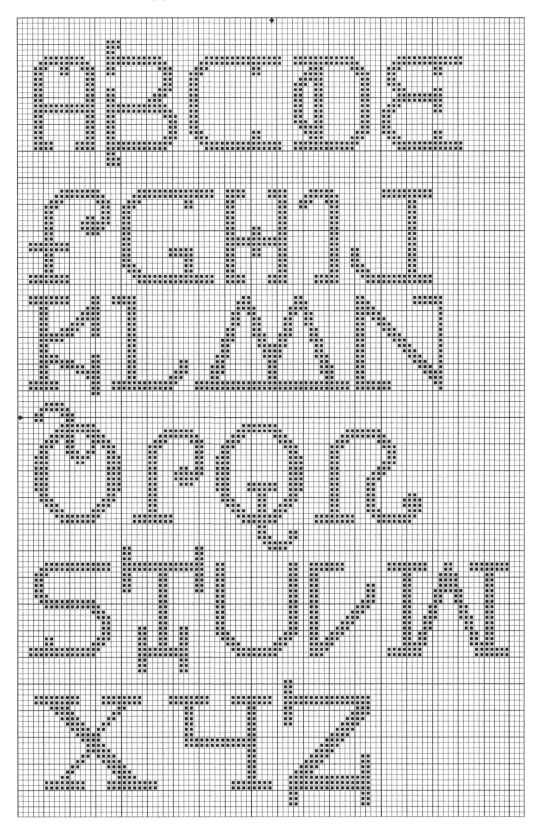

Buttercreme18 Lower Case

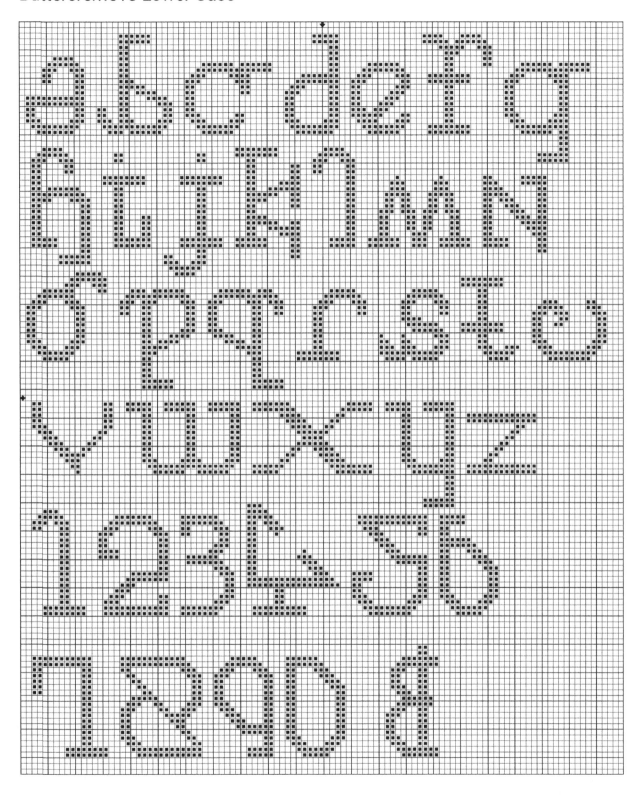

Buttercreme24 Upper Case   Graph 1 of 2

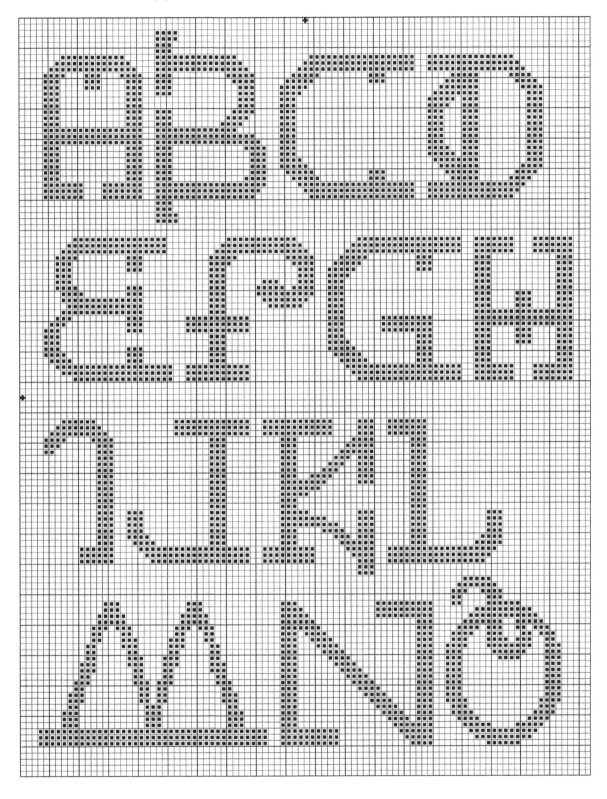

Buttercreme24 Upper Case　　　　Graph 2 of 2

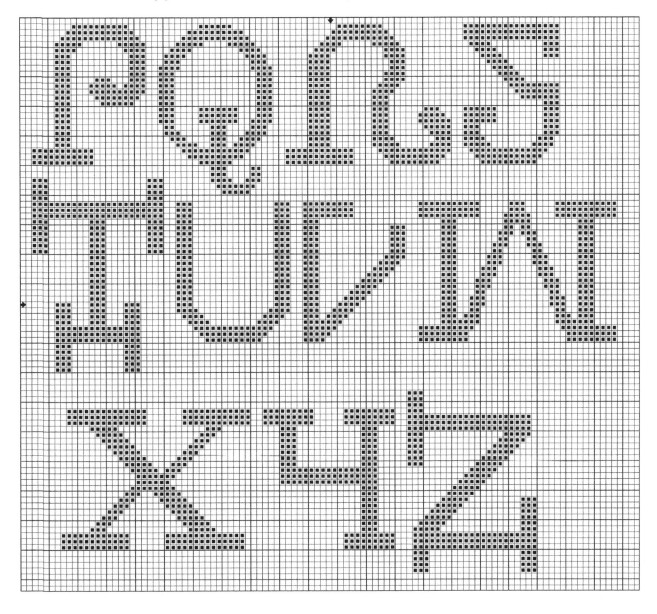

Buttercreme24 Lower Case   Graph 1 of 2

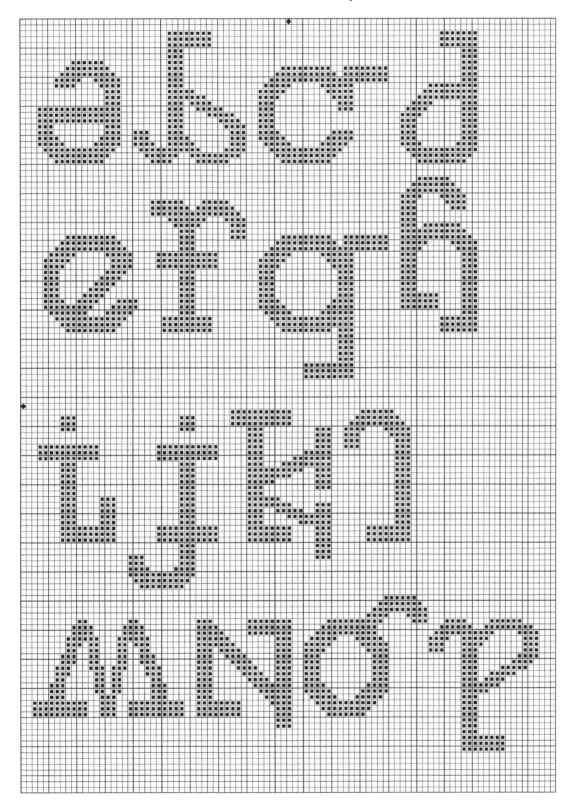

Buttercreme24 Lower Case   Graph 2 of 2

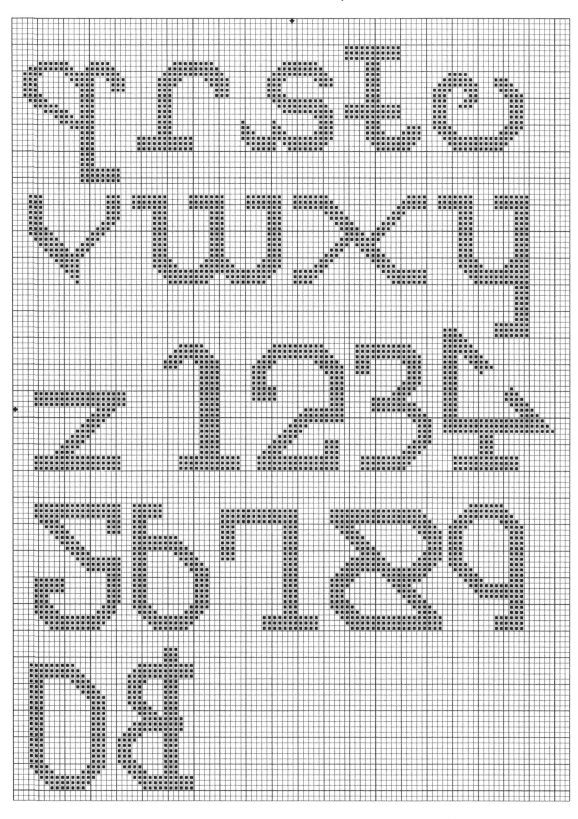

HoppieDown18 Upper Case

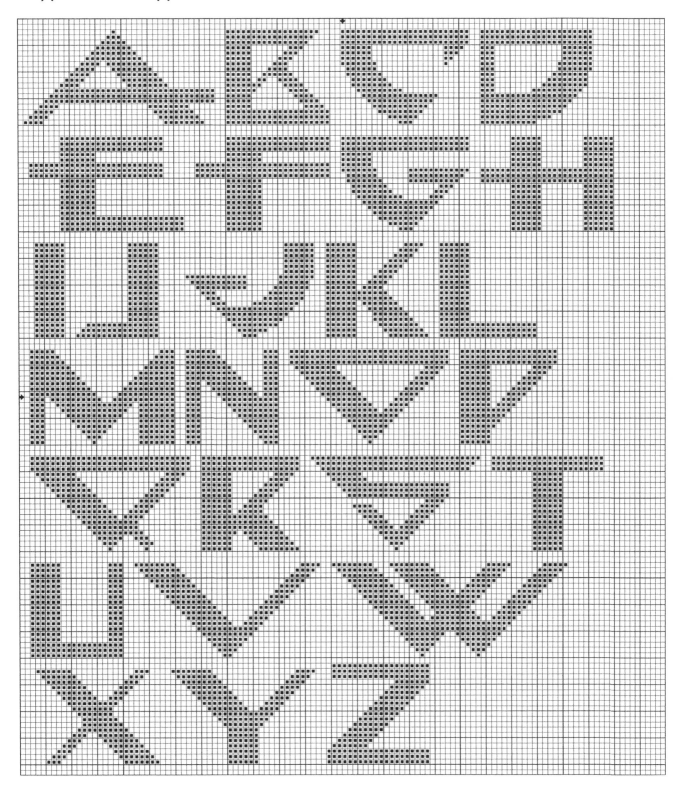

HoppieDown24 Upper Case   Graph 1 of 2

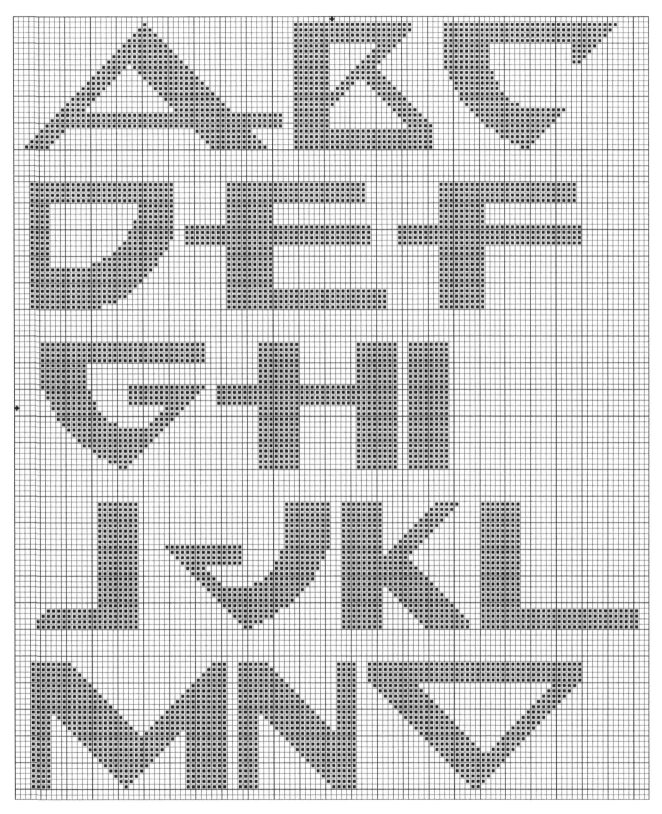

HoppieDown24 Upper Case   Graph 2 of 2

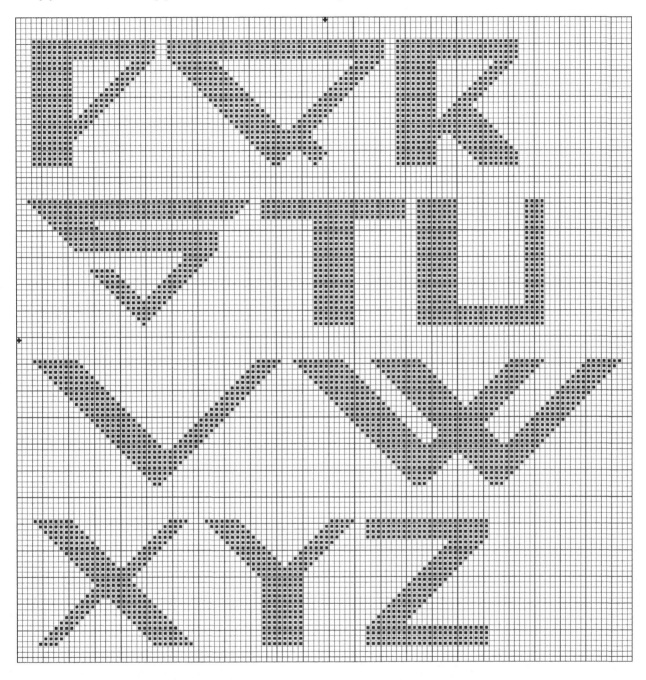

HoppieUp18 Upper Case

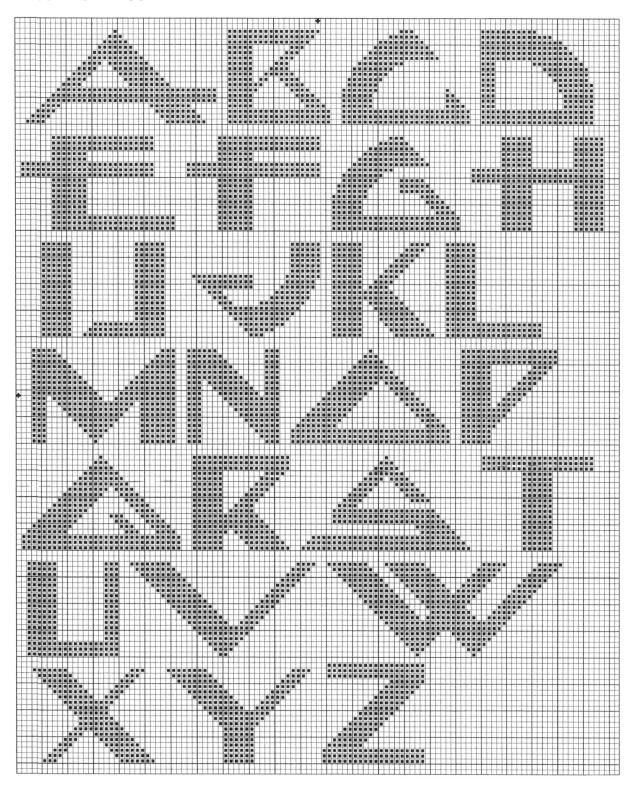

HoppieUp24 Upper Case   Graph 1 of 2

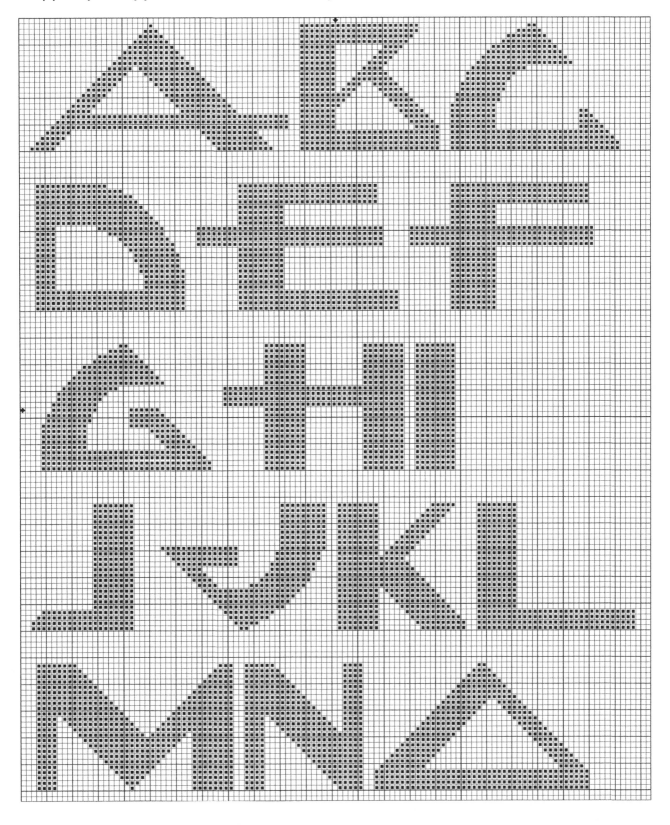

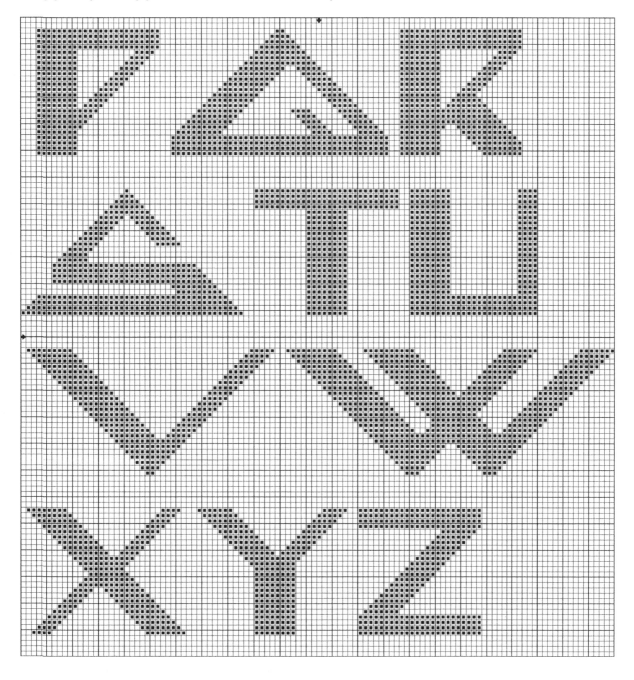

LicketyNotSplit18 Upper Case

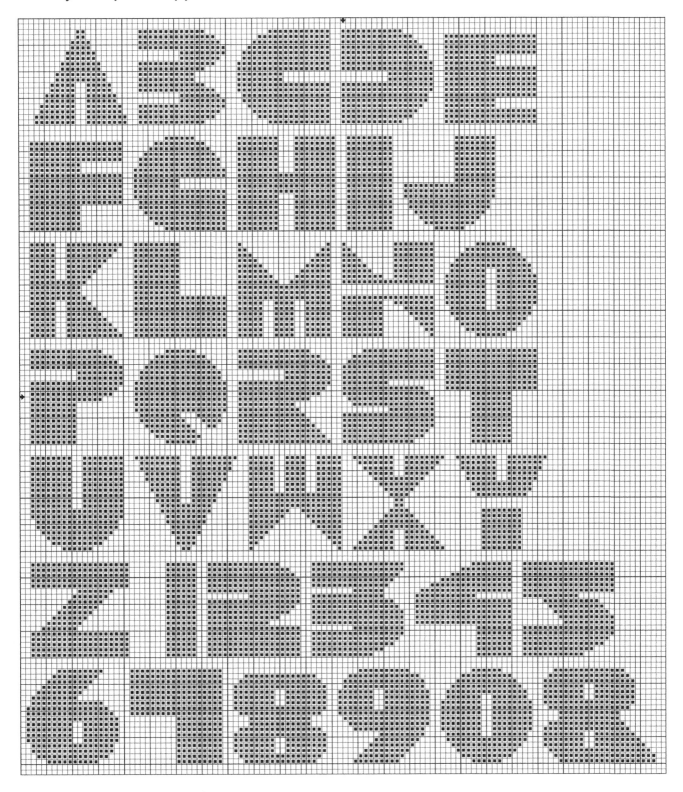

LicketySplit18 Upper Case

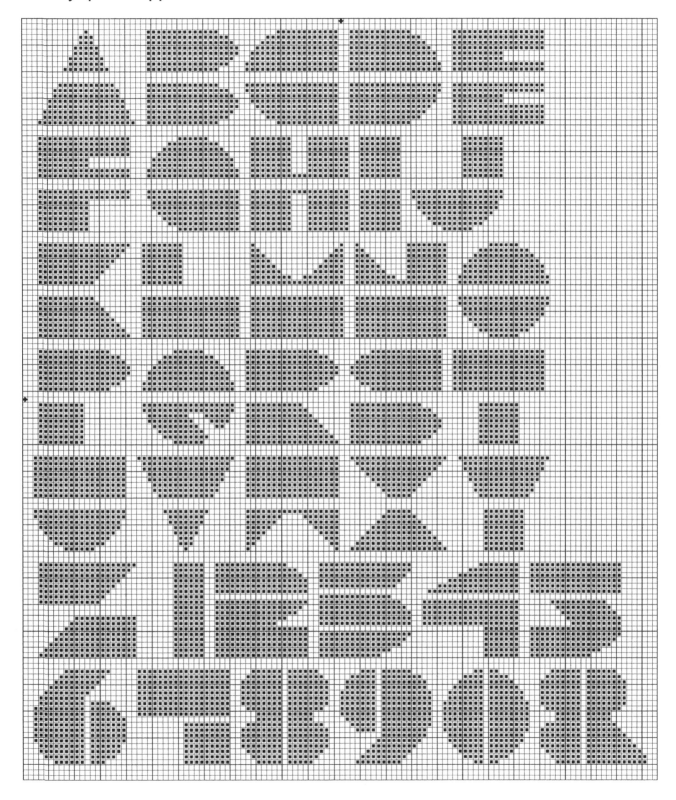

Mudgie18 Upper Case

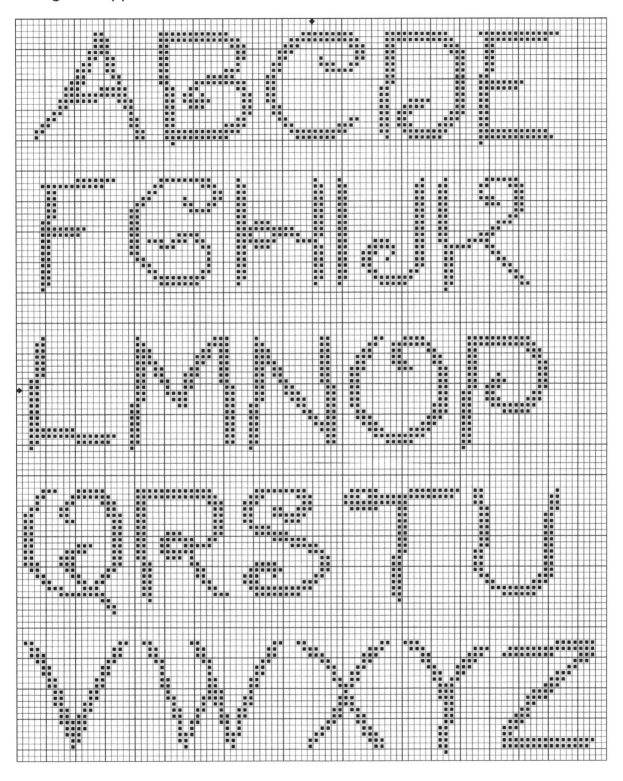

Mudgie18 Lower Case

Mudgie24 Upper Case   Graph 1 of 2

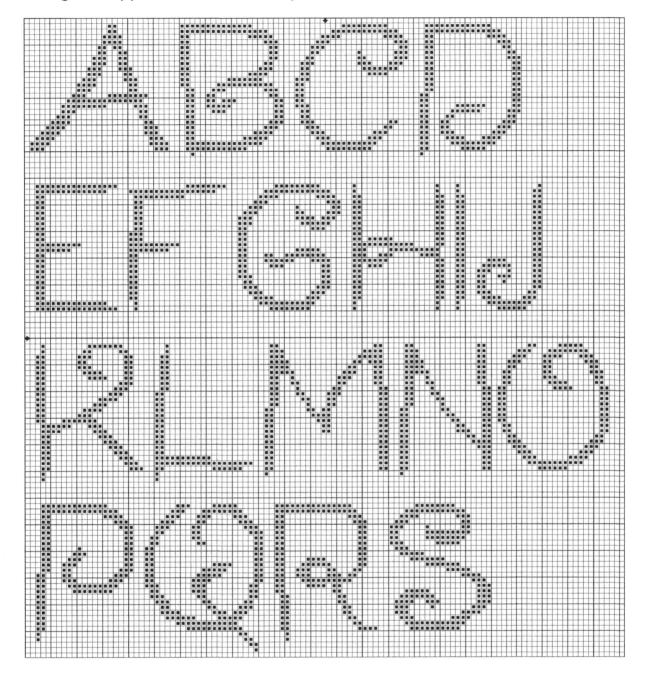

Mudgie24 Upper Case   Graph 2 of 2

Mudgie24 Lower Case

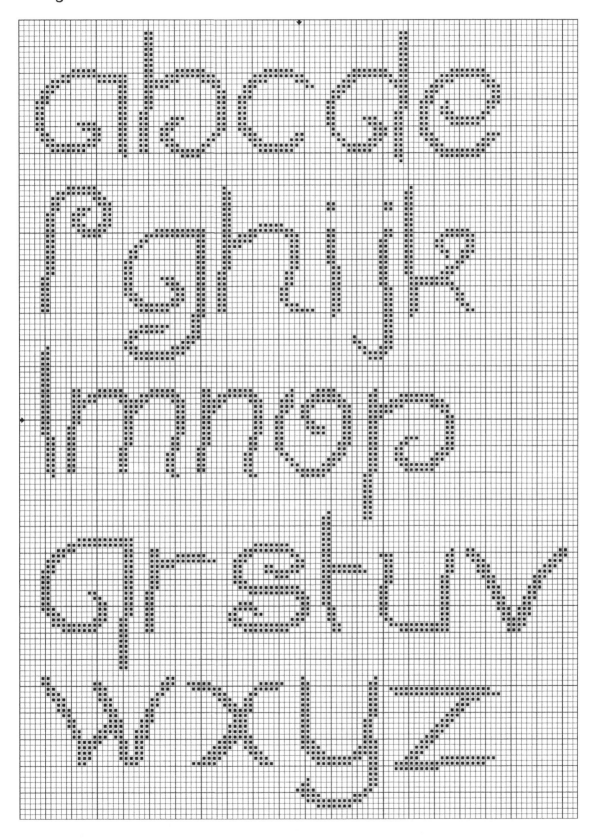

Noire15 Upper Case

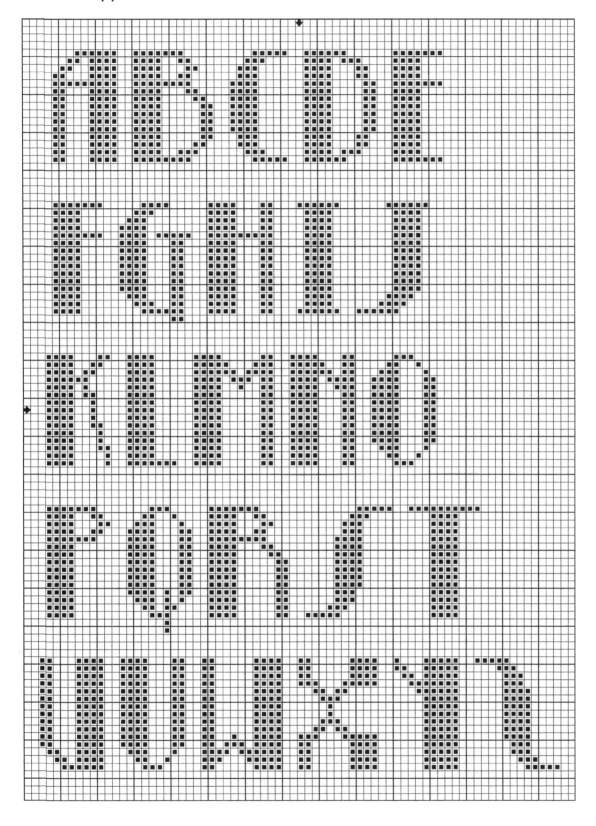

Noire18 Upper Case

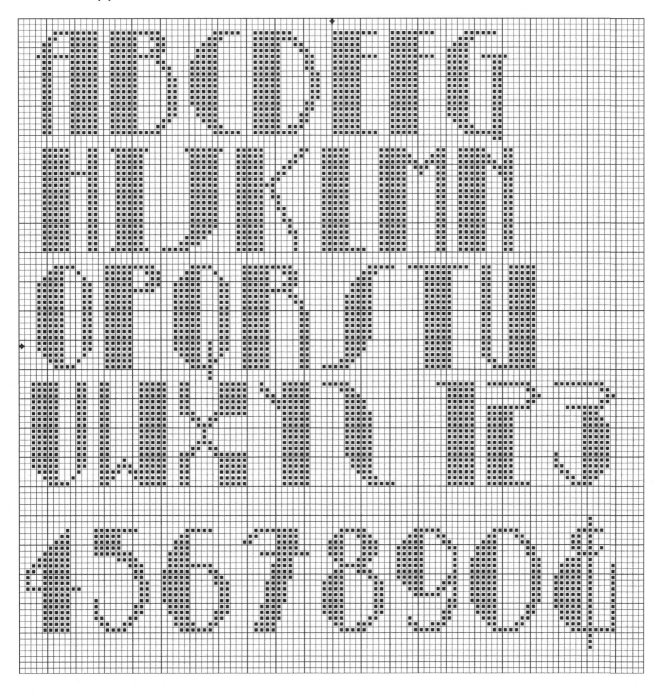

Noire21 Upper Case

Noire24 Upper Case   Graph 1 of 2

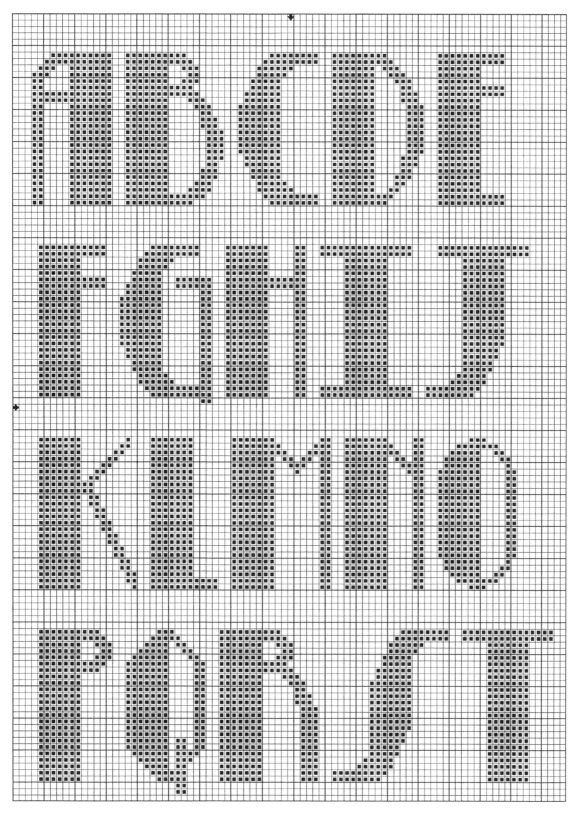

Noire24 Upper Case　　　　Graph 2 of 2

Seggie18 Upper Case

Seggie18 Lower Case

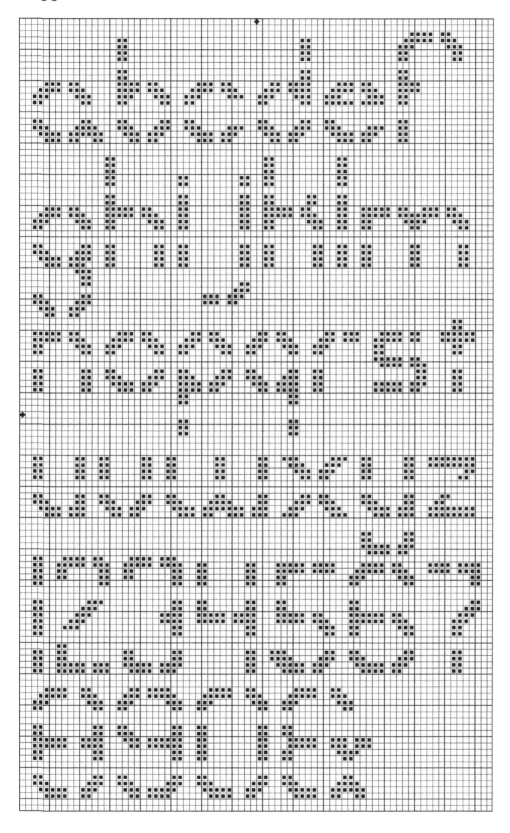

Seggie24 Upper Case

Seggie24 Lower Case

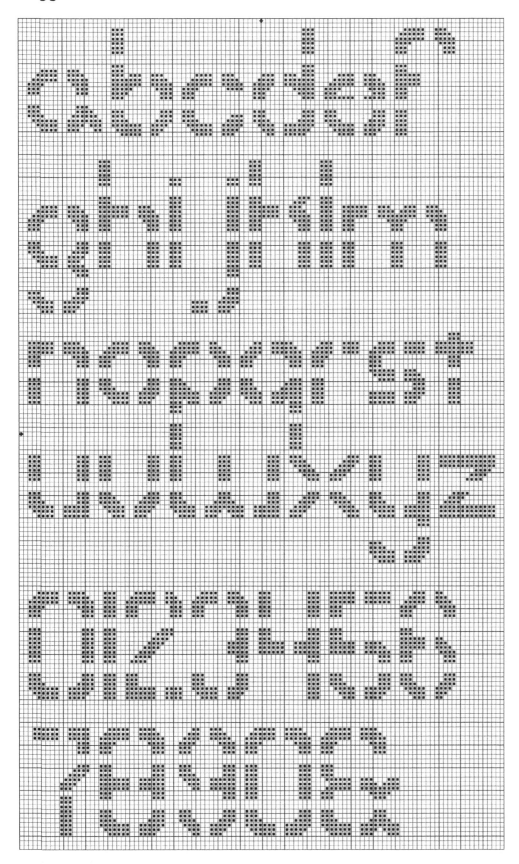

Threez18 Upper Case　　　　Graph 1 of 2

Threez18 Upper Case   Graph 2 of 2

Threez18 Lower Case　　　　　Graph 1 of 2

Threez18 Lower Case   Graph 2 of 2

Threez24 Upper Case   Graph 1 of 2

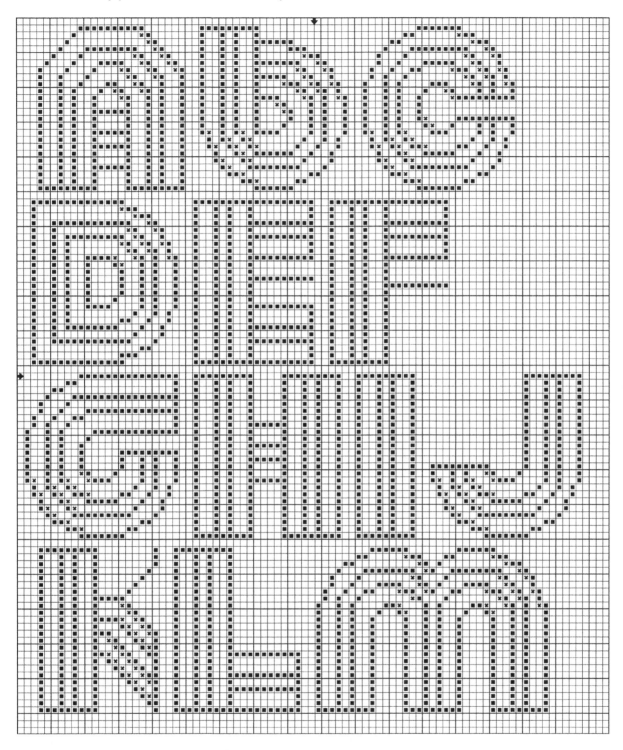

Threez24 Upper Case   Graph 2 of 2

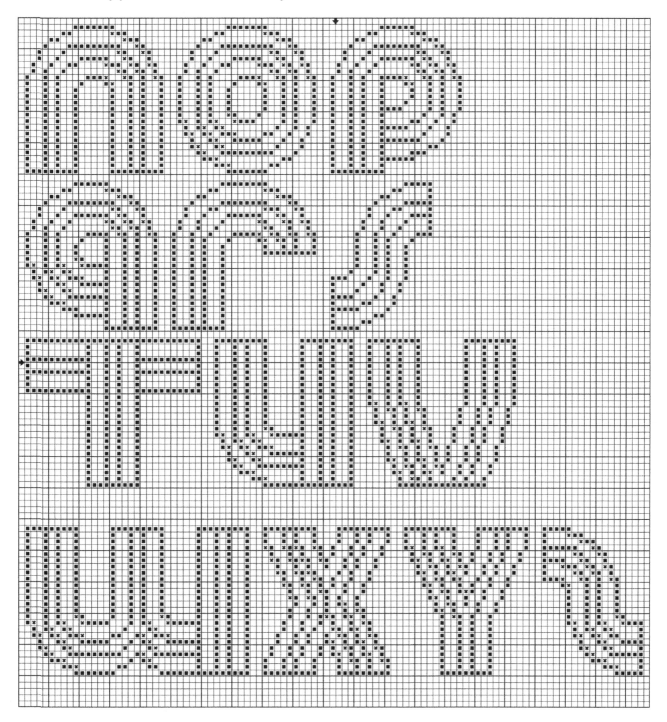

Threez24 Lower Case   Graph 1 of 2

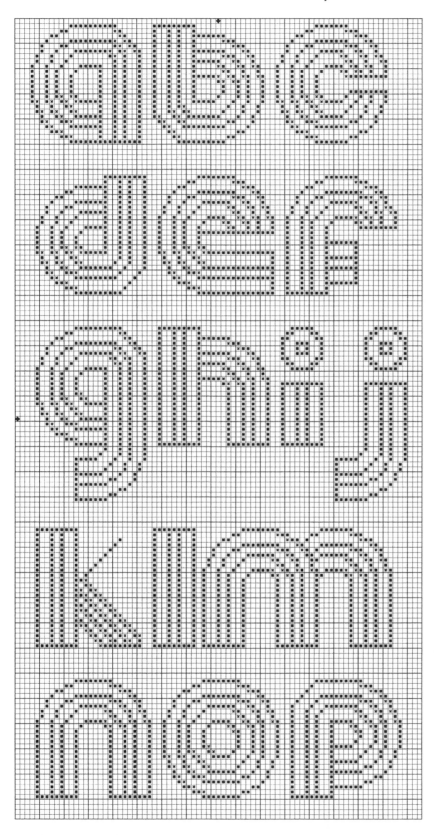

Threez24 Lower Case　　　　　　Graph 2 of 2

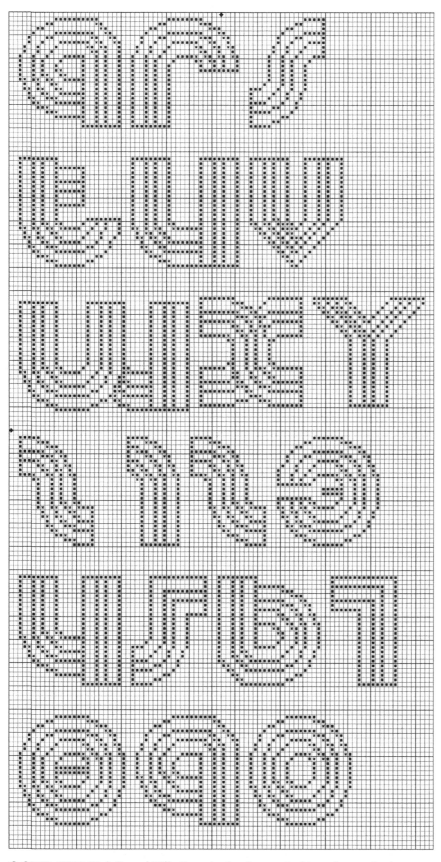

GRIDS
and
GRAPHS

20th ANNIVERSARY EDITION

TB-DN

ALPHABETS
For Discerning Makers

Grids and Graphs for Needlework and Crafts

HOW TO USE THE GRIDS AND GRAPHS

These *Grids and Graphs* allow you to create accurate charts for many needlework and craft projects. They can be used to create original designs or to modify existing designs.

There are 3 different types of Grids/Graphs depicted in here.

Square Graphs - These Graphs are designed to be *true size** and the heavy, dark lines fall at 1 inch increments.

> They are useful for Counted Thread techniques, such as **Needlepoint** and **Counted Cross Stitch**, which have ground fabrics with the same thread count vertically and horizontally.

> The Graphs are true size, so simply choose the Grid size which matches the ground fabric.

> Depending on your design needs, the squares can represent an individual stitch or each line can represent a thread of the ground fabric.

Beading Grids - These Grids depict the bead layouts for **Loom, Peyote, Two Drop, Brick,** and **Comanche Techniques**.

> Since beading projects can be quite small, these grids are not actual size but are proportionally accurate, allowing design work in an easily viewed size.

Ratio Grids - These Grids provide a wide range of useful options when working on a project where the horizontal units are a different size than the vertical units, such as **Knitting**, **Crochet, Weaving,** and **Smocking**.

> These Grids have heavy, dark lines every 5 lines, as a counting aid.

> The first number of the Ratio refers to the Horizontal Units and the second refers to the Vertical Units.

> Remember that you can always turn a Grid 90° to increase it usefulness. For example, if a project is 5 units horizontally and 4 units vertically, spinning the 4:5 grid 90° will result in that ratio.

Grids and Graphs for Needlework and Crafts

These Grids are proportionally accurate. Using the reduction and enlargement capabilities of copy equipment, the proper Ratio Grid can be sized to scale, as needed.

Tips for Success

When using the Graphs and Grids in this book, never write directly on the pages. Work on photocopies and keep the pages as clean as possible.

NOTE – Copy machines and printers may enlarge or reduce the image slightly, so when a true size copy is needed, measure it carefully and adjust it as needed.

For projects where the fabric will be created, such as **Knitting, Crochet, Weaving,** and **Smocking**, first create a 6" x 6" sample with the same techniques and materials that will be used in the design. Wash and steam the sample the same way the final project will be finished. Take careful measurements in each direction and find the Grid which is closest to those measurements.

The fewer stitches per inch a technique has, the more stitches the sample should have, to make it as accurate as possible.

Remember that a Ratio is the relationship between 2 numbers, reduced to the smallest increment. The initial relationship of Horizontal Units to Vertical Units may not seem to fit one of the Ratio Grids, but may be the same when reduced. For instance, a Knitting Gauge of 16 stitches to 20 rows is actually a 4:5 ratio. With experimentation, the Ratio Grids can be reduced or enlarged to a true working size.

If you need an area larger than what is depicted in a particular graph, tape multiple copies together to get the size needed.

Note: Permission is granted for the owner of this book to copy the Graphs and Grids for personal use.

SQUARE GRIDS - 12 x 12 GRID

20th Anniversary Grids and Graphs for Needlework and Crafts

SQUARE GRIDS - 13 x 13 GRID

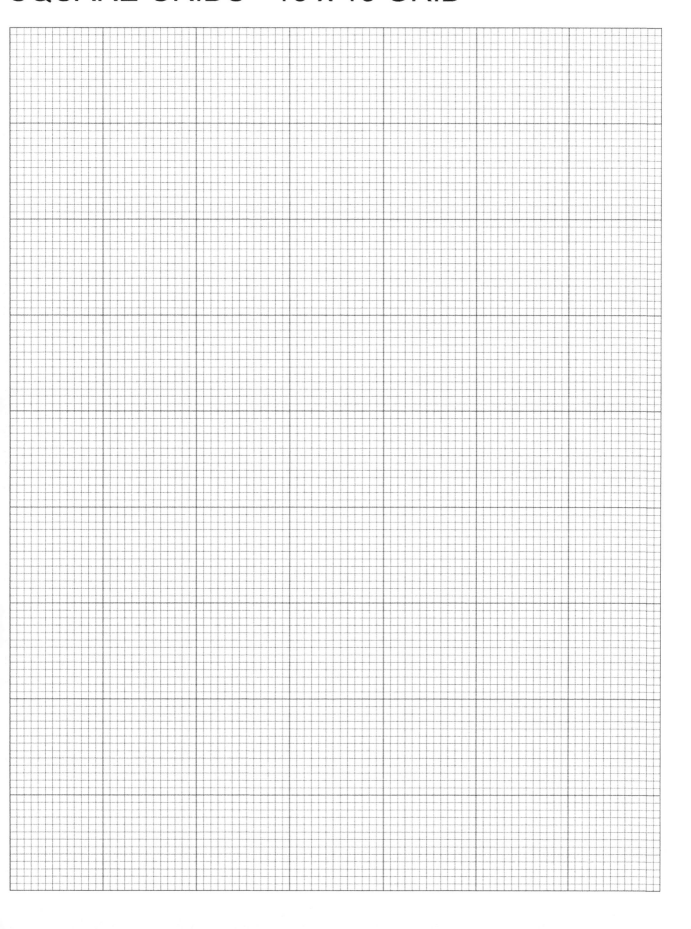

20th Anniversary Grids and Graphs for Needlework and Crafts

SQUARE GRIDS - 14 x 14 GRID

20th Anniversary Grids and Graphs for Needlework and Crafts

SQUARE GRIDS - 18 x 18 GRID

BEADING GRIDS - TWO DROP STITCH BEAD GRID

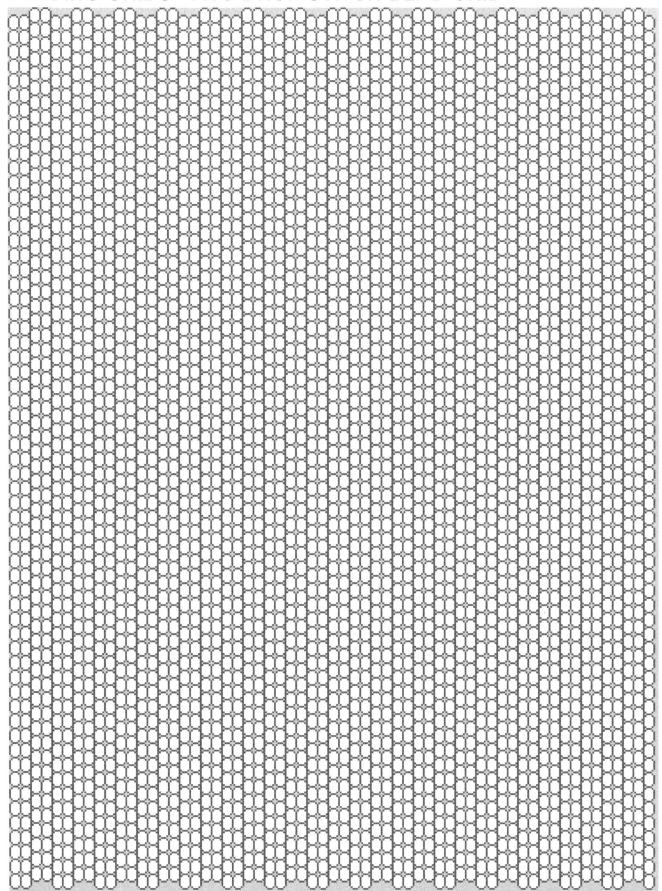

TWO DROP BEAD GRID

BEADING GRIDS - BRICK STITCH BEAD GRID

BRICK BEAD GRID

BEADING GRIDS - COMANCHE STITCH BEAD GRID

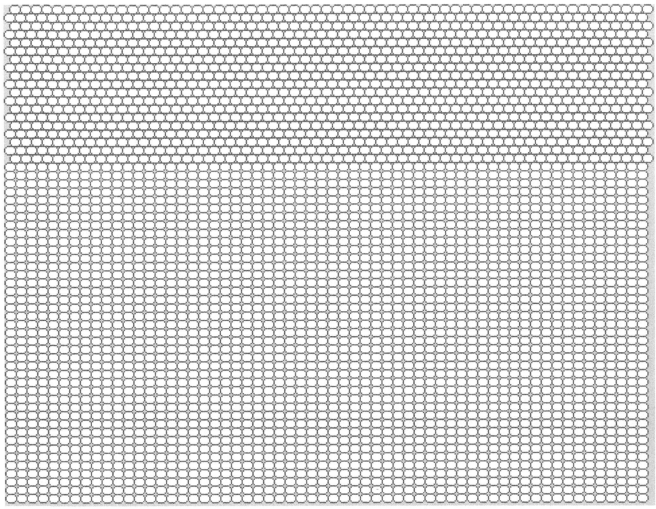

COMANCHE BEAD GRID

BEADING GRIDS - LOOM BEAD GRID

LOOM BEAD GRID

BEADING GRIDS - PEYOTE STITCH BEAD GRID

PEYOTE BEAD GRID

RATIO GRIDS - 2:3 GRID

20th Anniversary Grids and Graphs for Needlework and Crafts

RATIO GRIDS - 4:5 GRID

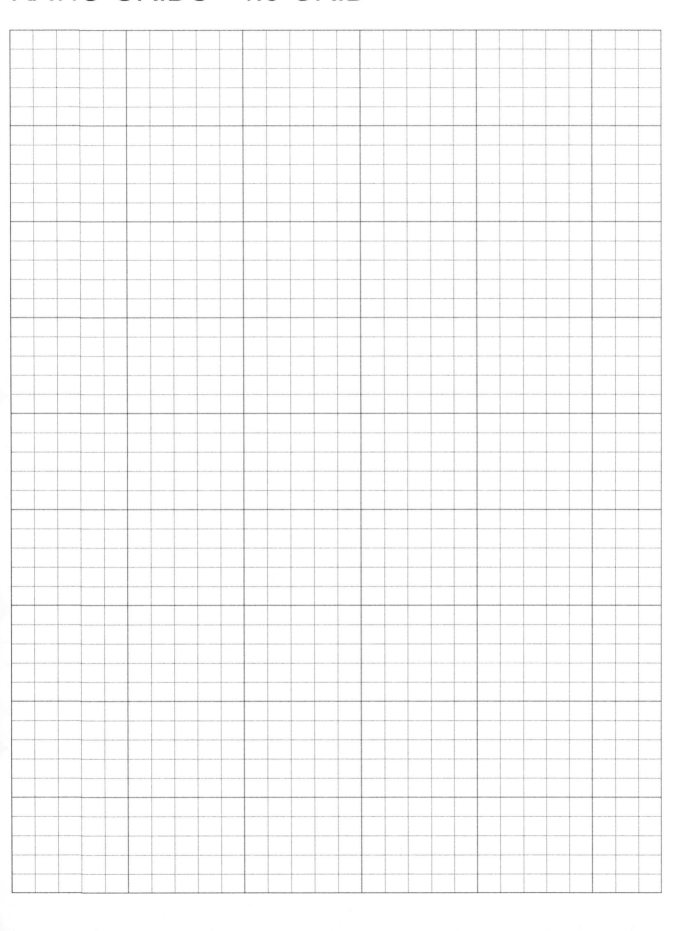

Other Titles Available from
TINK BOORD-DILL NEEDLEWORK
Available as PRINT or DIGITAL

Get FREE Alphabets

NEWSLETTER Sign-up at www.TinkBD.com/a

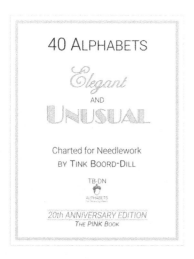

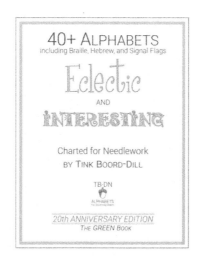

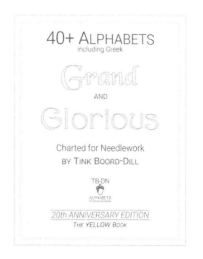

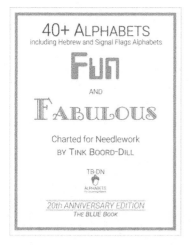

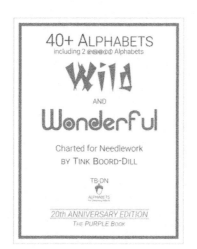

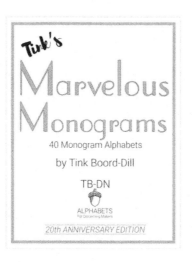

Made in the USA
Monee, IL
06 February 2022

90825219R00090